WHAT

HELP BATS SEE IN THE DARK?

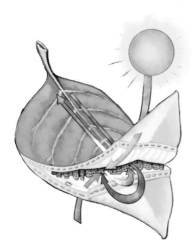

Om KIDZ

An imprint of Om Books International

Contents

Leaves are every plant's food factory! Plants use sunlight, water, carbon dioxide as ingredients to prepare food by a process called photosynthesis. But to trap sunlight, plants need a special ingredient called chlorophyll. Chlorophyll is a pigment which gives the leaves its green colour. Without leaves, most plants can't make food.

Pocket fact

Litres and litres of water!
The Baobab tree in Africa is known for its capacity to store water in its trunk. It can store 1,000 litres to 120,000 litres of water in its trunk.

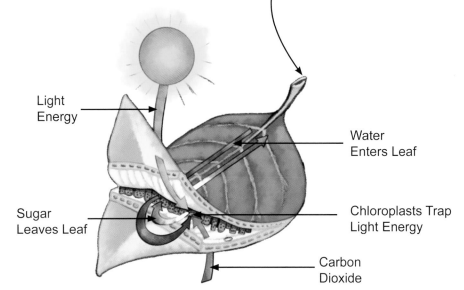

Light Energy

Water Enters Leaf

Sugar Leaves Leaf

Chloroplasts Trap Light Energy

Carbon Dioxide

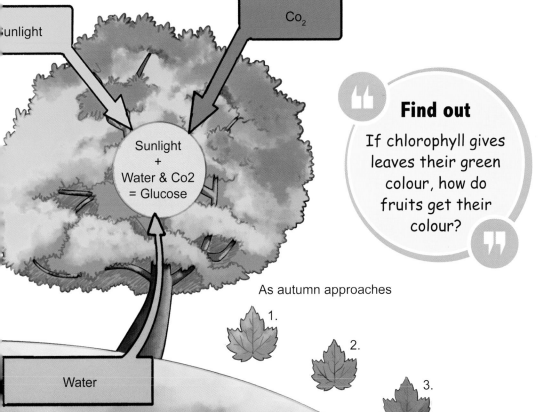

Sunlight

CO_2

Sunlight
+
Water & Co2
= Glucose

Water

As autumn approaches

1.

2.

3.

Find out

If chlorophyll gives leaves their green colour, how do fruits get their colour?

What makes leaves change colour in autumn?

Many trees don't get enough sunlight or water during the winter to make food and so they make and store food during the summer. In autumn, trees stop making food and don't need the chlorophyll, which gives the leaves the green colour. Chlorophyll disappears from the leaves and they turn red, orange, yellow and sometimes even purple.

What do plants do to protect themselves?

They have plenty of ways to defend themselves! Plants cannot run away when attacked, but don't be mistaken, they are not defenceless. They can protect themselves. Some plants have thorns that make it difficult to eat them. Others produce toxins that keep insects and animals away. Some have tiny hair on their leaves that stop insects from reaching the leaf's surface. Interestingly, some plants also produce odours when attacked!

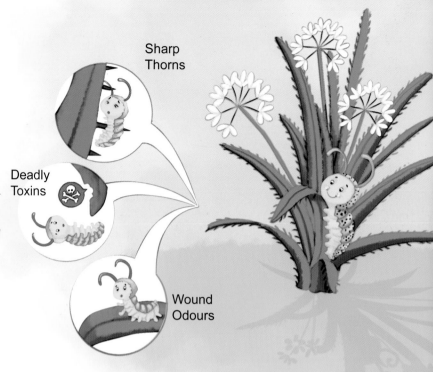

Sharp Thorns

Deadly Toxins

Wound Odours

Pocket fact

The largest flower in the world is the flower of the Puya raimondii. It has a flower stalk about 35,000 feet tall and bears over 8,000 white flowers.

Find out

Are flowers edible? Can you name a flower that can be eaten?

What makes flowers so colourful and scented?

Flowers come in vibrant colours like red, pink, blue, purple etc. due to a pigment called anthocyanins. On the other hand eugenol, ionones and many such chemicals present in the flowers give them their sweet scent. Flowers use both colour and scent to attract insects and animals that help them in pollination.

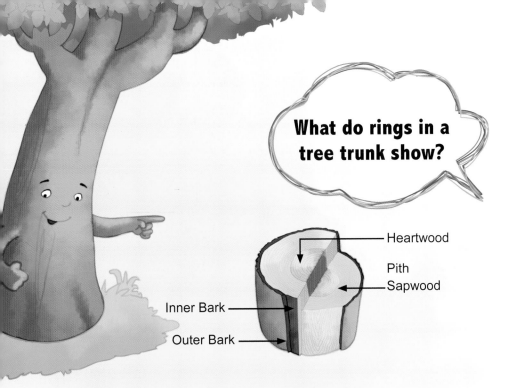

What do rings in a tree trunk show?

Heartwood

Pith

Sapwood

Inner Bark

Outer Bark

The rings on a tree's trunk show its age. A tree grows in two ways. The tips of its branches grow and make the tree tall. At the same time, roots, branches and trunk of a tree grow thicker. In every season, a new layer of wood is added to a tree trunk that appears as a ring. One ring signifies one year of growth, just like the candles on your birthday cake!

Find out

What is the similarity between radish, carrot and beetroot?

Pocket fact

I am 9,550 years old! The world's oldest living tree is in Sweden. Its root system is estimated to have been growing for 9,550 years.

What makes potatoes grow underground?

Potatoes are actually tubers or swollen stems! Plants often make extra food and store it away. A potato plant does something similar. There are tubers on the roots of a potato plant and as the plant makes extra food, it stores it in these tubers under the ground.

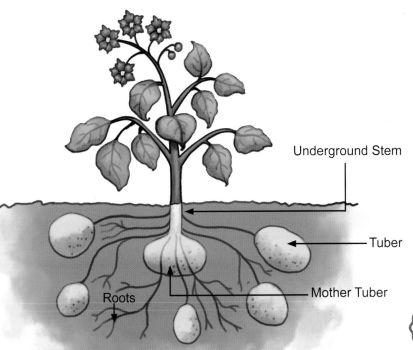

Underground Stem

Tuber

Roots

Mother Tuber

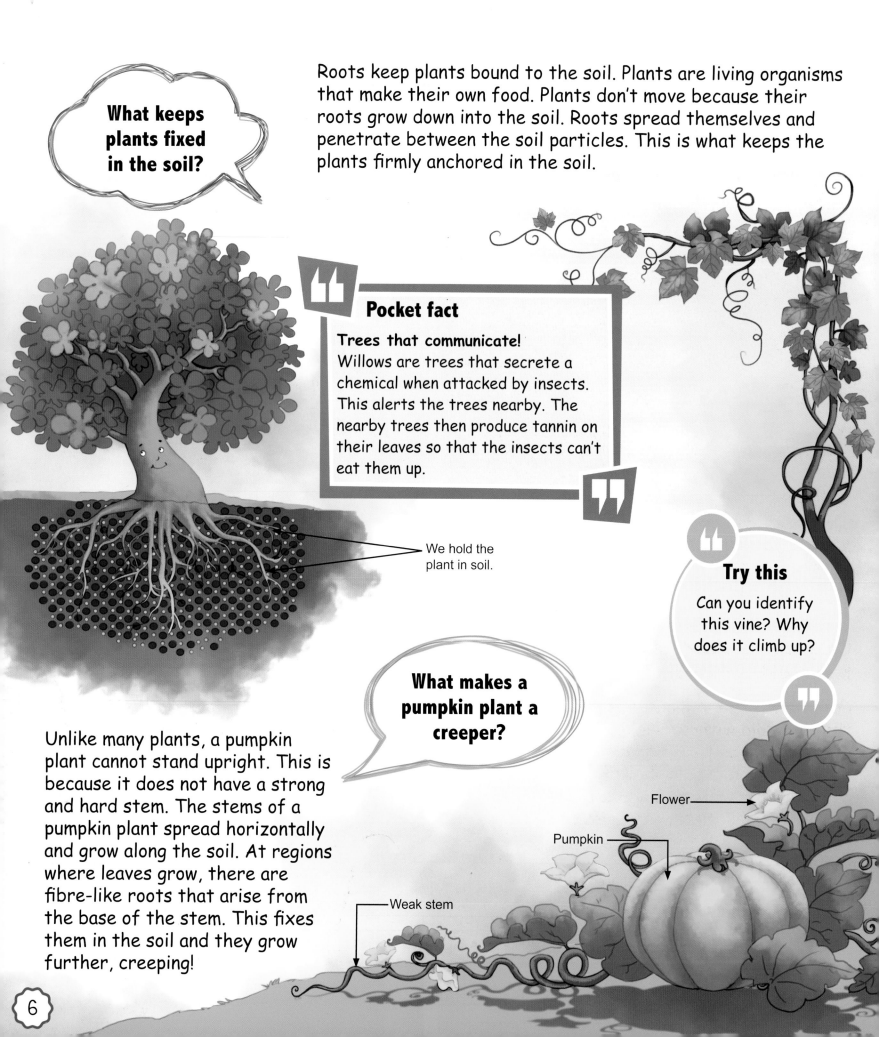

What keeps plants fixed in the soil?

Roots keep plants bound to the soil. Plants are living organisms that make their own food. Plants don't move because their roots grow down into the soil. Roots spread themselves and penetrate between the soil particles. This is what keeps the plants firmly anchored in the soil.

Pocket fact

Trees that communicate!
Willows are trees that secrete a chemical when attacked by insects. This alerts the trees nearby. The nearby trees then produce tannin on their leaves so that the insects can't eat them up.

We hold the plant in soil.

Try this

Can you identify this vine? Why does it climb up?

What makes a pumpkin plant a creeper?

Unlike many plants, a pumpkin plant cannot stand upright. This is because it does not have a strong and hard stem. The stems of a pumpkin plant spread horizontally and grow along the soil. At regions where leaves grow, there are fibre-like roots that arise from the base of the stem. This fixes them in the soil and they grow further, creeping!

Flower

Pumpkin

Weak stem

What makes lemons sour?

Lemons contain a weak organic acid called citric acid found in many fruits and vegetables. Fruits that contain citric acid are called citrus fruits. This citric acid is what gives lemons their sour taste. Interestingly, citrus fruits are rich in vitamin C too.

Rich in vitamin C

Pocket fact

Cashew nut shells may not be good for you but the poisonous shell liquid of cashews is good for many industrial uses, like friction linings, paints, and resins.

Find out

Can you name a vegetable that has citric acid and is juicy?

What keeps cashew nuts from being sold in shells?

Cashew nuts are yummy to eat but they are sold without shells, which are toxic. As cashew nuts grow, they develop a double shell that contains a poison called anacardic acid. This shell protects the inside from insects. The toxic coating is the reason that these yummy nuts are not sold in their shells like pistachios or peanuts. Instead, cashews are dried and roasted to remove their shells before they are sold!

Cashew Fruit

Cashew Nut

…helps bats see in the dark?

Bats 'see' in the dark using a special skill called echolocation, simply put, echo. They make a high-pitched noise with their mouth or nose and release sound waves into the air. The sound waves hit insects or objects and bounce back, creating an echo. From the echo it hears, the bat can detect objects and also how far they are.

Bat sonar

Returning sound waves

Pocket fact

The largest known bat colony in the world is the Bracken Bat Cave in Texas. More than 20 million bats live in the cave. It is more than the number of people living in Mumbai, one of the world's largest populated cities.

Try this

Identify this insect. I have a 'worm' in my name, I give you a type of cloth. Can you guess who am I?

Pad

Claw

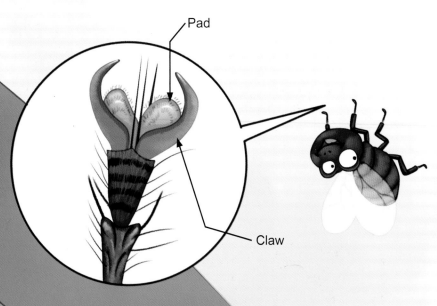

What makes flies sit upside down on ceilings?

Flies land upside down on a ceiling because of their special sticky feet! Flies also have footpads with tiny hair that help them stick to the ceiling. In addition to gummy feet, flies also have a special toe-like claw on each foot, which is used to pry themselves free!

What tricks do ants use to communicate?

Ants release a special type of chemical called pheromones. When other ants smell this chemical, they follow this scent trail to the food. At the same time, this scent also helps them protect each other and their young ones. Ants also use touch to communicate. They rub their antennae and front legs on their fellow ants to get their attention!

Pocket fact

A giant colony!
A giant colony of Argentine ants was discovered in Europe. It stretched to around 6,000 kilometres, posing a threat to animals and crops.

Find out

What other animals can live in a desert? Do all have features that can help them survive there?

What helps camels survive in a desert?

Camels have a thick insulating coat that protects them from heat during the day and cold at night. They have wide, padded feet so that they can walk in the sand without sinking. Camels have the unique ability to store fat in their humps and water in the lining of their stomachs, which can be used in times of need. Hairy eyelashes, ears and slit nostrils protect camels from dust and sand. With these features, camels can easily survive in the desert.

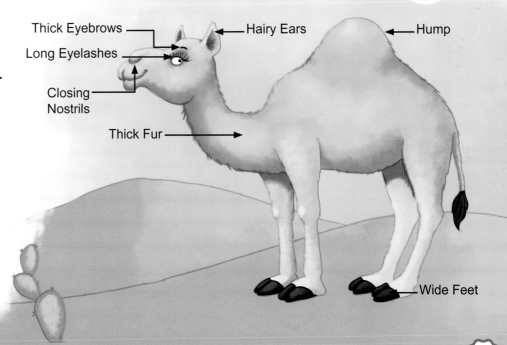

Thick Eyebrows — Hairy Ears — Hump — Long Eyelashes — Closing Nostrils — Thick Fur — Wide Feet

What causes sea breeze?

On a warm summer day along the coast, the heating of land and sea gives rise to local winds called sea breezes. Air above the land is heated by the Sun; it expands and rises as it is lighter than the surrounding air. Cool air rises above the sea's surface, replacing the warm rising air. This circulation of air is the sea breeze, which gives a pleasant cooling influence on hot summer afternoons!

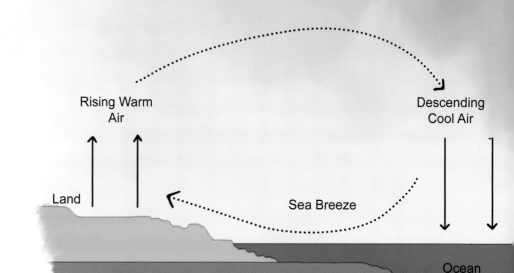

Rising Warm Air

Descending Cool Air

Land

Sea Breeze

Ocean

Find out

Can you name the different forms in which water falls from the sky? One example is snow.

Pocket fact

The greatest rainfall that was recorded in a day was at Reunion in the Indian Ocean. It occurred on March 15, 1952 and was 73.62 inches!

What makes rainclouds black?

Rainclouds are black because of their thickness and density. Clouds are made up of tiny drops of water. When drops are tiny, they scatter all colours of sunlight and appear white. A cloud gets thicker and denser when it gathers more water droplets. Like any object that transmits light, the thicker it is, the lesser light passes through it. As clouds get thicker, they scatter less light which makes them appear grey or black.

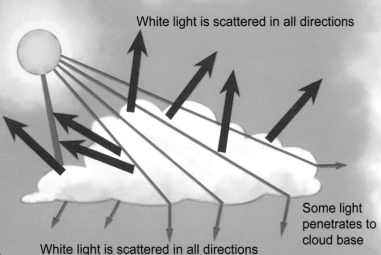

White light is scattered in all directions

Some light penetrates to cloud base

White light is scattered in all directions

What makes lightning appear in the sky?

Clouds collide and lightning appears! Lightning is a big electric spark. When a thundercloud is up in the atmosphere, bits of ice are formed. These tiny bits of ice bump into each other as they roll around in the air. This collision creates positive and negative electric charge. Positive charges, gather at the top of the cloud, while negative charges settle at the bottom. When these negative charges connect with positive electrical charges on the Earth, there's a zap of lightning!

Negative Cloud Bottom

Push

Negative Earth Bits away from Surface

Pocket fact

So many rainy days!
Mount Wai'ale'ale on Kauai, Hawai is recorded to have the most number of rainy days in a year. In a year, it has up to 350 rainy days!

Find out

Why shouldn't you stand under a tree when there's a lightning?

Cloud

Sun

Rain

What causes rain?

Clouds bring rain to us. Clouds are made up of tiny droplets of water that hold on to each other. Sometimes these tiny droplets bump into each other and become big. This makes the cloud heavy and Earth's gravity pulls these heavy drops down to the ground. And you hear the pitter-patter of raindrops!

What causes the Sun to rise and set?

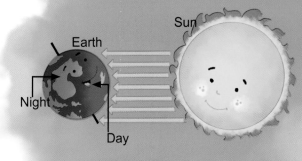

The Sun is at the centre of our solar system. It doesn't rise and set, but appears so because of the Earth's rotation on its axis. Earth makes one complete turn on its axis in 24 hours. As the Earth rotates from east to west, it looks like the Sun is moving in the sky.

Pocket fact

The coldest place!
The coldest continent on our planet is Antarctica. Once, Antarctica recorded a temperature of 52.7 degrees Celsius below zero!

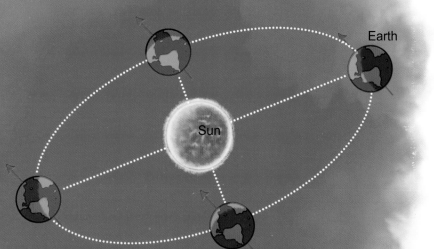

What causes seasons on Earth?

Seasons represent the changing relationship of the Sun and Earth. The Earth spins on its axis and at the same time, it also revolves on its orbit around the Sun. The Earth completes one revolution around the Sun in 365 ¼ days. While orbiting, different regions of the Earth receive different amount of sunlight during the year which causes seasons to occur!

What makes hurricanes so powerful?

Hurricanes are strong ocean storms. They are formed over warm ocean waters and sometimes, even strike land and can cause huge floods. Hurricanes get stronger when they are over warm ocean water surrounded by moist air that speed the storm. They also get strength from wind shear that disrupts them.

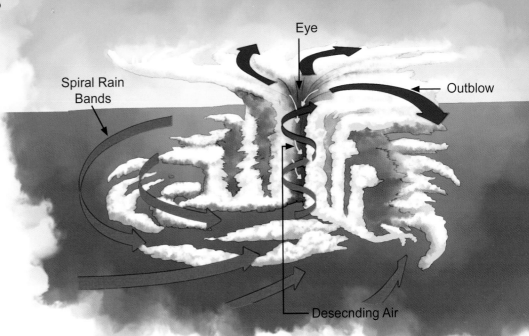

Pocket fact

In 2005, Hurricane Katrina killed over 1,800 people in the United States. It damaged property worth $80 billion. Around 80 % of the city of New Orleans was flooded and it was one of the worse-hit cities.

Find out

Which is the saltiest water body on Earth?

I have dissolved salts in me

What makes sea water salty?

Salts from the rocks on land make sea water salty. How? The rainwater that falls on the land is slightly acidic due to carbonic acid present in it. As the rain erodes rocks on land, acids in the rainwater break down the rock. This process creates ions that are carried away to the ocean. Ninety percent of the dissolved ions in seawater are chloride and sodium. Together they give ocean water the 'salty' taste.

What is lava?

Lava is molten rock that erupts from a volcano. It is formed deep beneath the Earth's surface where the temperature is very hot. Lava is called magma when it's underground. Eventually, some magma makes its way to the Earth's surface and escapes through a volcanic eruption. When magma erupts onto the Earth's surface and begins to flow, it is called lava.

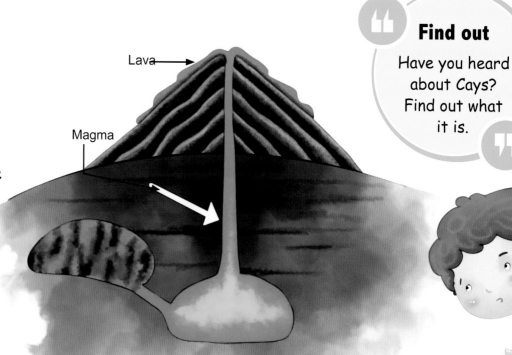

Lava

Magma

Find out

Have you heard about Cays? Find out what it is.

Pocket fact

Islands may not always be natural. Some islands are manmade too. The Kansai Airport in Japan rests on a manmade island.

What keeps islands from sinking?

An island is a piece of land surrounded by water on all sides. They are not floating landmasses but areas of the Earth, like an underwater mountain, that are raised up out of the water. This explains why islands don't sink in water.

What is a coral reef?

Coral reefs are large structures found in oceans and seas. They are made of the skeletons of marine animals called corals. The skeletons get deposited one over the other and make a large coral reef. Corals that build coral reefs are called hermatypic, or hard corals. This is because they extract calcium carbonate from seawater and make a hard, durable exoskeleton that protects their soft, sac-like bodies.

Pocket fact

Waterfall under the ocean!
Other than on land, you can find waterfalls under the ocean as well. The largest under ocean waterfall is between Greenland and Iceland. It drops 11,500 feet which is three times the height of any waterfall on land.

Find out

Which is the largest coral reef in the world?

What is the depth of the ocean?

Oceans are gigantic bodies of salt water that cover almost $\frac{3}{4}$th of the Earth's surface. The average depth of the ocean is about 12,100 feet. The deepest part of the ocean is 36,200 feet deep. This part is called Challenger Deep and is located beneath the western Pacific Ocean in the southern end of the Mariana Trench, southwest of the US territorial island of Guam.

12,100 feet

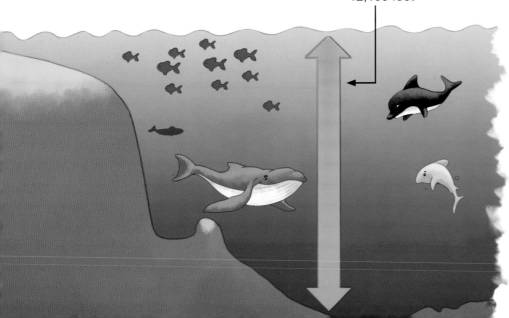

Index